W9-CPP-289

Eating Right

Mary Elizabeth Salzmann

Consulting Editor, Diane Craig, M.A./Reading Specialist

ABDO
Publishing Company

Published by ABDO Publishing Company, 4940 Viking Drive, Edina, Minnesota 55435.

Copyright © 2004 by Abdo Consulting Group, Inc. International copyrights reserved in all countries. No part of this book may be reproduced in any form without written permission from the publisher. SandCastle™ is a trademark and logo of ABDO Publishing Company.

Printed in the United States.

Credits
Edited by: Pam Price
Curriculum Coordinator: Nancy Tuminelly
Cover and Interior Design and Production: Mighty Media
Photo Credits: BananaStock Ltd., Corbis Images, Image Source

Library of Congress Cataloging-in-Publication Data

Salzmann, Mary Elizabeth, 1968-
    Eating right / Mary Elizabeth Salzmann.
        p. cm. -- (Healthy habits)
    Includes index.
    Summary: Explains in simple language the importance of eating nutritious foods in the right quantities.
    ISBN 1-59197-551-4
    1. Nutrition--Juvenile literature. [1. Food. 2. Nutrition.] I. Title.

RA784.S336 2004
613.2--dc22

2003057790

SandCastle™ books are created by a professional team of educators, reading specialists, and content developers around five essential components that include phonemic awareness, phonics, vocabulary, text comprehension, and fluency. All books are written, reviewed, and leveled for guided reading, early intervention reading, and Accelerated Reader® programs and designed for use in shared, guided, and independent reading and writing activities to support a balanced approach to literacy instruction.

Let Us Know

After reading the book, SandCastle would like you to tell us your stories about reading. What is your favorite page? Was there something hard that you needed help with? Share the ups and downs of learning to read. We want to hear from you! To get posted on the ABDO Publishing Company Web site, send us e-mail at:

sandcastle@abdopub.com

SandCastle Level: Transitional

Eating right is a
healthy habit.

Eating right helps you stay healthy and grow strong bones and muscles.

Eating a lot of fruits and vegetables is part of eating right.

Eating some meats, grains, and dairy products is also part of eating right.

Eating right means eating fewer fats and sweets.

Kay has a bowl of fruit for breakfast.

Lenny drinks milk
every day.

Jim eats a sandwich with vegetables for lunch.

Jay likes watermelon instead of cake for dessert.

What are your favorite foods?

Did You Know?

You have 206 bones in your body.

On average, a person eats over 66,000 pounds of food during his or her life.

An orange tree produces about 1,000 oranges each year.

More than 360 different kinds of cheese are made in France.

Gainesville, Georgia, is the Chicken Capital of the World.

Glossary

fruit. the fleshy, sweet part of a tree or plant that contains one or more seeds

grain. the seed of cereal plants, like rice and wheat

habit. a behavior done so often that it becomes automatic

muscle. the body tissue connected to the bones that allows us to move

vegetable. the edible part of a plant grown for food

watermelon. a large fruit that grows on a vine and has a hard, green rind and sweet, watery pulp

About SandCastle™

A professional team of educators, reading specialists, and content developers created the SandCastle™ series to support young readers as they develop reading skills and strategies and increase their general knowledge. The SandCastle™ series has four levels that correspond to early literacy development in young children. The levels are provided to help teachers and parents select the appropriate books for young readers.

Emerging Readers
(no flags)

Beginning Readers
(1 flag)

Transitional Readers
(2 flags)

Fluent Readers
(3 flags)

These levels are meant only as a guide. All levels are subject to change.

ABDO
Publishing Company

To see a complete list of SandCastle™ books and other nonfiction titles from ABDO Publishing Company, visit **www.abdopub.com** or contact us at:

4940 Viking Drive, Edina, Minnesota 55435 • 1-800-800-1312 • fax: 1-952-831-1632